NOT Selling Myself Short

ONE WOMAN'S JOURNEY
with
TURNER SYNDROME

About the Cover:

Sally had the pleasure of getting acquainted with a gentle camel named Malachi. She is shown with her Bible, reading a portion of The Creation Story from Genesis, in celebration of God's Creation of Animals! Along with Patty and Mike McKonly, who gave permission to use this photo. Malichi lives at Kleen Acre Farm near Columbia, Pennsylvania.

NOT SELLING MYSELF SHORT

ONE WOMAN'S JOURNEY *with* TURNER SYNDROME

SALLY WISNER OTT

XULON PRESS

Xulon Press
2301 Lucien Way #415
Maitland, FL 32751
407.339.4217
www.xulonpress.com

© 2021 by Sally Wisner Ott

All rights reserved solely by the author. The author guarantees all contents are original and do not infringe upon the legal rights of any other person or work. No part of this book may be reproduced in any form without the permission of the author. The views expressed in this book are not necessarily those of the publisher.

Unless otherwise indicated, Scripture quotations taken from the Holy Bible, New International Version (NIV). Copyright © 1973, 1978, 1984, 2011 by Biblica, Inc.™. Used by permission. All rights reserved.

Printed in the United States of America.

Paperback ISBN-13: 978-1-66280-952-1
Ebook ISBN-13: 978-1-66280-953-8

TABLE OF CONTENTS

Preface vii

Setting the Stage: 1

Getting to Know Me 3

Getting to Know about Turner Syndrome 5

Life's too Short to be Self-Critical. 9

Life's too Short to be Exclusive: 11

Life's too Short to Worry about
What We Cannot Control. 13

Life's too Short to be Concerned about
What Others Think of Us: 15

Life's too Short to Hold a Grudge: 17

Life's too Short to Compare Ourselves to Others: 19

Standing Tall 21

Feeling Supported 25

Responding to God's Call. 27

Living Through Ups and Downs 35

Reaching Out 39

Standing on the Promises. 41

Acknowledgements. 45

About the Author 47

PREFACE

*A*S A SPIRITUAL director, it has been my privilege to be one of the spiritual companions of Sally for the last few years. I have been enriched by the time we have spent together looking at how God is moving in her life. Spiritual companionship is a discipline that aids a person's spiritual formation through purposeful reflection upon everyday experiences which in and of themselves are filled with divine mystery. The writing of one's autobiography is another discipline, a type of examen prayer, reflecting upon where we have noticed God acting in our lives:

Every life is a gestalt of blessings that makes up each unique irreplaceable life. Every experience is a blessing that shapes us into the person God is creating us to be. This shaping had its beginning with the dawn of creation, the start of an evolutionary process that has brought us to this time and place. The hand of the Potter has shaped our clay and with joy has watched our lives take shape. Because no two lives are the same, in the sharing of our stories we grow in our humanity, our compassion, and our understanding of God. This us why it is important to remember and record our experiences. This gives us the opportunity to share our reflections on their meaning with others. It is God's desire to use them to gently touch and shape other lives not just now, but also in future generations.

In *Not Selling Myself Short: One Woman's Story of Her Journey with Turner Syndrome,* Sally has shared how her life has been shaped by the hand of God. As a woman of faith, she has shared how her life's experiences have been shaped by her faith and an awareness of God's love for her. Her story is a word of encouragement not just for women born with a condition that adds some unique challenges to life, but for all of us who are also born with other conditions that have added to the unique challenges we face in our lives.

It is my prayer that Sally's sharing will inspire you to reflect upon where God has been in your life's journey and that you will want to record and share them with others. It is in the sharing of our stories that we can gain perspective from our own lives, and enable others to gain a new perspective on theirs. May you be encouraged not to sell yourself short as you share in the life of Sally Wisner Ott.

Rev. Michael C. Johnson

SETTING THE STAGE:

EVERYBODY HAS A story. This is mine. My husband sometimes tells me, *"I know you like a book."* So I thought I would write one and see if he is right

My life began on August 23, 1948, when I was born to Beth and Harold Wisner, in Grand Rapids, Michigan. The youngest of three siblings, I came into this world with a genetic condition called Turner Syndrome.

> <u>What is Turner Syndrome</u>? It's a genetic condition which only affects females. Girls are typically born with two complete X chromosomes. Chromosomes come in pairs; one set from the mother; the other set from the father. While girls get 2 Xs, boys get an "X" and a "Y". Turner syndrome is the absence of all or part of the mother's second "X" chromosome, in some or all of the body's cells. Common syndrome features are short stature and lack of ovarian development, including menstruation, which typically begins for girls at around 12.

GETTING TO KNOW ME

ONE EVENING, WHEN I was six years old, my father took me to our local A&W for a root beer float. I had no clue that he orchestrated this outing to tell me that he would be leaving my mother. While I was too young to understand the issues in their marriage, I was *not* too young to understand that my father cared enough to tell me what was happening. He could have just walked away. Instead, he walked out, for about two months. To this day I remember waking up one morning to find him in our home again. He said while he was away, he remembered the good things and did not think as much about the bad.

Nowhere is it written that life should be easy. "Easy" is an illusion.

When I was 8 years old, my parents noticed that I had not grown any taller in an entire year. This did not concern me at the time, but Mom and Dad recognized that this was not typical for a child my age. We went to see my pediatrician in Grand Rapids, Michigan. He agreed that my lack of physical growth was not typical. His advice? *"You could go to the University of Michigan's Medical Center in Ann Arbor, but they might refer you anyway, so I suggest that you to Johns Hopkins Hospital in Baltimore, Maryland.*

With that, Dad and I set out on an adventure in search of a diagnosis. At this point, I, too, was becoming curious about why I was different than many/most of my friends. I was given nicknames like: Short Stuff; Pint-Sized; Little, but Mighty; Dynamite; Stretch; Little Bit and Shorty.

A highlight of our trip to Baltimore was traveling on the Pennsylvania Turnpike, through a few tunnels. I thought the tunnels were cool, never dreaming that I might live in PA. I also liked the umbrella tables outside the motel where we stayed one night. Dad bought me a paint-by-number set, so that I could enjoy being outside and being *somewhat* creative.

GETTING TO KNOW ABOUT TURNER SYNDROME

IT WAS AS a result of a series of tests at Johns Hopkins that I was diagnosed with Turner Syndrome. It is a condition which my Mother and Father had never heard of. I had never heard of it either. If you happen to share this diagnosis with me, I *really* want you to know that you are not alone.

One of the staff I met at Johns Hopkins was a child psychologist who explained that those unique individuals who have Turner Syndrome are typically unable to have biological children. After my appointment, Dad asked me, *"How did it go?"* I said, *"Dad, I have a problem."* Of course he was concerned. He wanted to know what that problem was! I told him we had talked about the option of adoption, and I told him my problem was, *"I can't decide whether I want to adopt 12 boys or 12 girls."* Yes, that's how my 8 year old heart and mind worked at the time.

Approximately 99 percent of fetuses with Turner Syndrome spontaneously terminate during the first trimester. The condition accounts for about 10 percent of the total number of spontaneous abortions in the United States. Yet here I am! This explains why my Turner Syndrome Society of the United States T-shirt says, "Be uniquely you." I need to remember, when I'm feeling "less than", that I'm actually a miracle!

<u>What Causes Turner Syndrome</u>? To date, TS is not known to be associated with anything in the environment. It's all genetic.

<u>How is Turner Syndrome Diagnosed</u>? Girls and women are diagnosed at various stages of life, even at the later months of a mother's pregnancy. As awareness of TS increases, the age of diagnoses decreases. Usually, there is something "different" about a female that prompts her parent(s), a doctor(s) or the woman or girl herself to investigate the possibility of TS.

Before birth, TS can be diagnosed by taking a sample of the mother's amniotic fluid, other fetal tissue, or blood to examine the types of chromosomes. An Ultrasound, which provides a picture of the fetus, is also used. This helps to screen patterns like for fluid buildup around the neck, and kidney or any indication of heart issues.

After birth, TS can be diagnosed by taking a sample of blood or other tissue from the infant. Because there are a range of health, developmental, social, and learning challenges which might affect girls and women with TS to different degrees, early diagnosis is critical. Identifying the syndrome as soon as possible helps doctors to determine whether the girl or woman has related health issues that need treatment or monitoring.

<u>Physical Characteristics and Related Health Conditions</u> – Each individual with TS is unique – and special! There are, however, some characteristics which are linked to TS, such as: Short stature. Another characteristic is not being able to get pregnant or give birth.

Turner syndrome is not life threatening. It can, however, be connected to a variety of other medical and developmental issues. In addition to those mentioned above, I have hypothyroidism (an underactive thyroid gland); I have early hearing loss; I have celiac disease, requiring a gluten-free diet; I have challenges with perception. (This has made math my most difficult subject.) Fortunately, I am not currently challenged by kidney or heart defects, though some with TS do live with these challenges as well.

Fortunately, my personal health issues are being regulated by diet and/or medication. One personal challenge I had with perception involved driving an SUV. I wanted this car, but I could not see well over the hood. I sometimes misjudged how much room I needed in a parking lot or to park on the street. I also seemed to underestimate how much room I needed when maneuvering some turns. Because of this, two of my husband's friends told him that he should take my keys from me, because I shouldn't be driving. I'm extremely grateful that he didn't. We're both grateful to a car salesman who has become a good friend and was able to intervene in this situation. He didn't judge me when a series of mishaps occurred. Some were just dings, while others caused more noticeable damage. He agreed that I should be driving a smaller car, and he helped us find a vehicle which is a much better fit for me.

TS occurs in 1 out of 2.000-4000 females. In the United States, around 70,000 women are thought to have TS. Growth hormone therapy (Estrogen) is the primary treatment. I began taking hormones at age 12 and continued this therapy into my 50's, when the time came to discontinue it.

I have Turner Syndrome. It does not have me. Yet it is a significant part of who I am.

Living in a unique body has prompted me to value the gift of life, to be drawn to the Power of Positivity, and to reflect on ways to expand upon the phrase **"LIFE'S TOO SHORT TO ..."** I invite you to do the same as I share my thoughts.

LIFE'S TOO SHORT TO BE SELF-CRITICAL.

Self-criticism, or self-downing, is an indicator of low self-esteem. This a struggle for many who live with TS. At times I find myself taking stock of who I am and what I'm doing, which leads to asking myself, *"Why me? Surely there is someone else who could do this better than I."* On the other hand, my Spiritual Director has consistently said, *"God looked at all the people who could be doing what you are doing, and said, 'I choose Sally'".* In one session he said, *"Through Turner Syndrome, God has given you some special gifts."* One of the gifts of this unique condition is that I've come to accept being unique. Being short is the way I was created.

LIFE'S TOO SHORT TO BE EXCLUSIVE:

$\mathcal{I}$ AM A SENIOR Adult who stands 4 feet 8 inches tall. I know what it's like to be overlooked. As a child at recess, when captains picked their teams for kickball, volleyball, softball etc., I expected to be one of the last, if not <u>the</u> last choice. As a teen, I often spent weekends and other free time with girlfriends, rather than dating.

My father taught public speaking, first in high school, then in college. He also judged forensics contests and spoke at special events, like high school graduations. When visiting in his classroom, I got to witness his art of teaching. After a student presented a speech, he would ask his class, *"What did you like about this speech?"* Following the responses, he then asked. *"How can we help your classmate to improve as a public speaker?"* He was kind to his students! He often went "above and beyond" by counseling them, when requested. His students were inspired by his compassion. I learned how to care for others from my father.

God has blessed me with an INCLUSIVE spirit. As a result, I try to avoid overlooking or excluding others! I am persuaded that God is the Creator of all persons. I am persuaded that all persons are created with Sacred Worth.

LIFE'S TOO SHORT TO WORRY ABOUT WHAT WE CANNOT CONTROL

*D*URING THE SUMMER following my sophomore year in high school, my parents separated again. This time they divorced. It shocked them when, after overhearing their argument one day I said, *"Why don't you two get a divorce?"*

There was no physical or verbal domestic violence in our home. Yet there was a lot of tension. They answered my question by letting me know that they were trying to stay together until I graduated from high school. They did not want to make life difficult for me, especially with my school friends. I told them, *"Well, you're not helping me if you can't get along."*

I could not control my parents' relationship with each other. What I could control was my reaction. So many things happen in this life that are beyond our control. I'm thinking of the weather; traffic; health issues; and how other people respond to us. I try *not* to spend a lot of energy worrying about the things that are beyond my control, because I believe this is not an effective use of energy.

My father had an interesting take on worry. He liked to tell this story: "*Someone once said, 'Don't tell me it doesn't help to worry. 90% of the things I worry about never happen.'*"

My faith has taught me that worries are often temporary and draining, On the other hand, HOPE springs eternal! In lieu of worrying. I believe it's a more productive use of time and energy is to use the resources of my faith. For me, this involves reaching out to others who have the knowledge and/or experience to help me to accept and/or let go of what I cannot control.

LIFE'S TOO SHORT TO BE CONCERNED ABOUT WHAT OTHERS THINK OF US:

I WAS IN AWE of my mother's beauty and talent. As a seamstress, she made most of my clothes. She also had a striking soprano voice and often sang solos in church. I learned about structuring my activities from my mother. I admired her gifts. In addition to being talented, my mother also faced challenges. She was sometimes depressed and self-critical. She was a perfectionist who became upset when things didn't go well.

As a child, I tended to take on the moods of my mother. If she was happy, I was happy. If she was sad, I was sad. I didn't want to disappoint her. It wasn't until I became an adult that I understood how difficult growing up had been for her. One day she said to me, *"Mother* (my grandmother) *always loved her plants more than she loved her kids."* Our relationship improved as I became more aware of her brokenness!

My sister was five years older than I, and my brother was a year younger than my sister. I came along came along four years later. As I was growing up, I sometimes felt like a nuisance to them. I was concerned about what they thought of me. My sister was married when she was 16, and my brother was extremely independent. Our family life was rocky, which taught me the value of coping with adversity.

There was a time in my life when I was almost consumed by people pleasing. I know now that I was way too focused on getting everyone to like me! During this time, my father actually said to me, *"Everybody loves Sally."* At the time, his affirmation felt *really* good! As I've matured, I've learned that there are some exceptions to this rule. It's just not realistic to think that *everybody* could, would – or even should – love me! In college, as a major in sociology and a minor in social work, I learned that trying to please others and wanting to "save the world" tend to be occupational hazards for social workers.

My husband and I like browsing in gift shops. In one shop, a refrigerator magnet caught my eye. We left without it. When I could not get it out of my mind, I asked if we could go back so I could purchase this magnet. It says, *"You can't make everyone happy. You are not a cupcake!"*

LIFE'S TOO SHORT TO HOLD A GRUDGE:

I AM AWARE OF only one time when I was denied employment because of my size. During my college years I was active in the Wesley Foundation, our United Methodist Campus Ministry. The Director of the church camp which I attended as a youth came to Wesley to recruit summer staff. Having precious memories as a camper there, I scheduled an interview and was excited about the possibility of a summer job at "my" church camp.

The Manager was kind, as well as candid. After getting acquainted, he said, *"I'm sorry, Sally, but I can't hire you."* I figured that I would have been working in the kitchen. I was right. He explained that their kitchen staffers worked with very large pots and pans, hung out of my reach and too heavy for me to handle.

Thankfully, I had a Wesley Foundation friend who was aware of my disappointment with the results of this interview. He said, *"It's okay, Sally. You don't want to work in a kitchen, anyway. You want to work at the camp where I am the Director, where you will be a counselor of children and youth."* He knew that I am more relational than task oriented. I worked at this camp for three consecutive summers. Though the pay was "nothing to write home about", there were many rewards. Fortunately, not getting the first job did not lead to holding a grudge. Being a counselor was a better fit for me than working in a kitchen.

I wonder ... Is there anyone who has not, at some time, been disappointed, or even hurt, by the words or actions of others? This hurt, when extreme, can lead to verbal and/or physical abuse. Have you ever heard the phrase, *"Hurt people hurt people"*? I believe that this is true.

So, how I would respond in a helpful and encouraging way to a person who has been deeply hurt? This would depend on the individual and on the particular situation, of course. I would definitely make an effort to communicate that holding a grudge often damages us more than those who hurt us, intentionally or unintentionally. I might ask the one who is hurting what I often ask myself, *"Is it possible that you are overreacting and being hard on yourself? I suspect that it might make a significant difference if you were kind and loving to yourself".*

When you or I fail to forgive another person (perhaps by deciding *not* to forgive) for doing or saying something damaging, it may hurt them for a while. But it affects us/me just as much. and potentially for a longer period of time. Holding a grudge doesn't make us strong. It makes us bitter. Forgiving doesn't make us weak. It sets us free.

LIFE'S TOO SHORT TO COMPARE OURSELVES TO OTHERS:

Galatians 6:4 says, *"Do your own work well, and then you will have something to be proud of. But don't compare yourself with others."*

WHEN I JOINED a local church staff as Pastor of Visitation and Outreach, there was a sign on the building's outdoor bulletin board which said, **"Be yourself. Everyone else is taken!"**

In a life changing conversation with a parishioner of a church that I previously pastored, I compared myself to this church's former pastor, a woman whom I will always admire. This parishioner interrupted my lament by saying, *"You don't have to compare yourself with anyone. You know,* **"comparison is the thief of joy.""** Prior to this conversation, another friend had advised me, *"Sal,* **don't let anyone steal your joy!"** Great advice!

STANDING TALL

THE GOOD NEWS for people of all shapes and sizes is that God touches our points of shortness and says to us, "STAND TALL!" Sometimes this encouragement comes from other people. There was the time that I went to Park City to buy a pair of pants for my husband. He's slender and slightly short for a man, so I usually have to look for a while to find his size. That day I found *one* pair in the size and color he wanted. Guess where they were? On the very top shelf! I looked around for a step stool, or a person taller than I who wasn't already occupied. The clerks were all busy at their registers, and there was not a step stool to be found. Finally I noticed a couple who were checking out. They were both tall. While the man was paying for their purchases, I asked the woman if she would mind reaching the pants for me. When she smiled and said, "Sure," I knew I had asked the right person. She seemed pleased to be able to help.

One day my Spiritual Director said, *"I'll bet you can relate to the Biblical story of Zacchaeus."* He was correct! The most obvious way in which Zacchaeus felt short was that he couldn't see Jesus in the midst of a crowd. But there were other ways, too. He knew that he was cheating the people from whom he was taking taxes. He was SHORT of friends. He was materially rich, but poor in spirit. So he decided to climb a tree. Maybe then he could see Jesus. Through this encounter, he regretted being a cheater, he wanted to correct the injustice of his ways, and he was given the opportunity to return the money he had unjustly and illegally collected.

There are things in our lives which make it difficult for us to see Jesus. There are things that crowd in to clutter up our lives. That's the bad news. The good news is that recognizing the things that are crowding in on us and keeping us from seeing Jesus is the first and most important step in dealing with them and being able to see Jesus more clearly.

To experience the full impact of Zacchaeus' story, we need to know that his story is not just about physical shortness. It's about transformation. Zacchaeus was transformed by his encounter with Jesus. That part of the story raises *some* important questions upon which I've been reflecting:

- ➢ What are <u>you</u> searching for?
- ➢ How and where are <u>you</u> searching? and
- ➢ Are <u>you</u> willing to be transformed by the process of searching?

Because we're human, it can be tempting to give in to our short points, our points of weakness. It can be tempting to hide somewhere, maybe even climb a tree. That's the bad news. The good news is in the way Jesus relates to us during those times, making it possible for us to change. It's Jesus' nature to say, *"C'mon now. Come down out of that tree. You don't have to hide. In fact, I'm going home with you today."* The good news is, regardless of how I'm feeling about myself, whether I'm feeling high or low, or somewhere in between, I know that I am not alone. The good news is I don't have to set myself apart in order to see Jesus. I am a child of God. It doesn't get any better than that!

I wonder ... What are the points of shortness in <u>your</u> life? As we seek to learn and to grow, we all have times when we struggle to STAND TALL. To be honest, there are times when I feel short of a number of things: energy ... patience ... enthusiasm ... confidence ... talent ... wisdom ... time. Of course, I'll always fall short of perfection. In those times I can't say that I totally appreciate being short.

We live in a society which tends to value tallness. In some circles, tall and thin is "in". Since I was curious about where this comes from, I decided to check the dictionary definitions of the contrasting words, SHORT and TALL. Webster says SHORT means, "<u>NOT</u> COMING UP TO STANDARD." Then we turn to TALL and it doesn't say "NOT SHORT." It says, "HIGH IN STATURE". I'm grateful that I get to live my life, not just according to dictionary definitions, but according to Biblical standards and the definitions of Jesus.

During my years in youth ministry, I met a Christian songwriter and retreat leader who impressed me with his understanding of the definitions of Jesus. His name is Jim Manly. One of his songs is called "Dance". I especially appreciate the chorus:

Tall people are gorgeous, and short ones are neat,

Skinny or bulgy, each body's a treat.
So dance as you are, you were made by the One
Who calls you to be what you've only begun ...

There are some specific lessons for ALL of us from Zacchaeus' story, regardless of our age, gender, ethnic background, or physical stature:

Jesus touches our spots of shortness and says to us "STAND TALL!"

Jesus accepts the socially unacceptable, the people who are marginalized by our society.

Jesus' love is more than a privilege bestowed upon those who are strong. It's a source of strength for those who are week.

Jesus had a way of helping *everyone* to feel encouraged. I believe that to strive to follow Jesus' example give us the potential to make a significant difference.

FEELING SUPPORTED

I GET EXCITED WHENEVER another person tells me, *"You make me feel so tall."* It gives me an opportunity to say, *"I figure that helping other people to feel tall is a worthwhile mission in life."* I have fond memories of one Sunday when I was the guest preacher at a church near my home. When the pastor invited me to join him in greeting the people following the service, a woman about my size asked her pastor, *"Would you take a picture of the two of us?"* My colleague picked up his camera. As we were getting ready for this "Kodak moment," (a dated phrase, I know ... but I'm over 70.) A third woman said, *"Wait! I want to be in this picture, too!"* I didn't ask either of my new friends if they were familiar with T.S. It was enough just to know that we felt connected because we were similar in size.

When I preached at another church, following the Benediction, as we were transitioning into a social time in their fellowship hall, a young adult approached me with an amazing smile. She gave me a big hug and said, *"Oh my gosh, you're so cute!"* I'm hoping that she might have heard at least *a bit* of my message, but I won't worry about that too much. Again, the important thing is we connected!

In one of many trips to see my family and friends in my home state of Michigan, I visited my sister, who lived in a high rise for senior citizens at the time. Sharon asked, *"You don't mind if I show you off a bit, do you?"* She had told her neighbor, Barb, about me, and Barb had said, *"I want to meet your sister."* When Barb opened her door, I was greeted by a woman who was maybe an inch or two taller than I. She hugged me and said, *"Sit down and tell me all about yourself."* Wow!

RESPONDING TO GOD'S CALL

UNDERGIRDING MY UNIQUE life story is a deep and abiding faith in God. Psalm 139:1-7 feeds my soul:

You have searched me, Lord, and you know me.
You know when I sit down and when I rise;
you perceive my thoughts from afar.
You discern my going out and my lying down;
you are familiar with all my ways.
Before a word is on my tongue you, Lord, know it completely.
You hem me in behind and before,
and you lay your hand upon me.
Such knowledge is too wonderful for me, too lofty for me to attain...

Psalm 139:13-14 says, *"For you created my inmost being; you knit me together in my mother's womb.*

I praise you because I am fearfully and wonderfully made;"

When I was 12 years old, my parents and my home church provided the opportunity for me to attend church camp for the first time. This experience showed me that God is *so* much bigger than what was going on in my own church and community. I was delighted to make new friends from many other churches. Another highlight of this experience was meeting a couple who were serving as missionaries in Malaysia. I noticed how they smiled, how they laughed, how they sang, and how they prayed. This was the planting of a seed that maybe God could do something special with *my* life. I returned to church camp every summer until I graduated from high school. I spent my first 3 summers after high school as a camp counselor. My call was confirmed over and over again – with a subtle, but significant change. As a 12 year old, I assumed that being a missionary meant moving to another country, perhaps even another continent, adapting to a different culture, and possibly learning at least one other language. As I matured, it became clear to me that there is a tremendous need for missionaries here, in my own country of origin.

After graduating from Western Michigan University in Kalamazoo, Michigan, I learned of a mission opportunity for young adults. It was called the US-2 program. Persons accepted into this program serve for two years with a mission agency within the USA. I was assigned to the staff of Lessie Bates Davis Neighborhood House in East St. Louis, Illinois. East St. Louis is an area of dire poverty. Serving as a US-2 raised my awareness that diversity is evidence of God's Creativity and it taught me that agencies such as Neighborhood House depend on the support of mission-minded individuals, including mission-minded pastors and congregations.

The next step in my faith journey was being introduced to Eden Theological Seminary, across the river in St. Louis, Missouri, by a colleague and mentor who has been a companion in my spiritual journey since the early 1970's. Upon entering the main building on Eden's campus, a poster on a prominent bulletin board caught my eye. It was a cartoon of Ziggy, with the caption, *"Just when I think I've discovered where it's at ... Somebody moves it!"* I thought to myself, "I belong here!" I was given a tour of the campus by a senior student, in addition to meeting with the Dean of Students. I asked him, *"Do you have a Master of Arts in Social Work degree?"* He replied, *"We do. However, I advise students, especially women, to pursue our Master of Divinity Degree. You can do everything with a Master of Divinity Degree that you can do with a Master of Arts Degree, but the reverse is not true.* This was definitely sound advice! At the time I was a young adult, and not sure that I would be pursuing Ordination. This visit to Eden included attending a chapel service. The theme was "Loving Faithfully in the Midst of Tension." The "take away" for me was that it is often easier to live at one end of a continuum (i.e. between freedom and responsibility), than to live in the tension along the continuum. To this day I strive to think in terms of "both/and", rather than "either/or."

I remained on the staff at Neighborhood House for a total of 4 years before graduating from Eden with a Master of Divinity degree.

After several years of serving in pastoral ministry, and six years of serving as Youth & Camping Coordinator in the Yellowstone Conference, UMC (Montana & Wyoming) and 2 years as Program Minister at First UMC in Billings, MT., I experienced a challenging period of inner restlessness. This lasted for about a year and a half. I would wake up in the middle of the night thinking. "I'm not sure I can be a pastor for the rest of my life." At first it wasn't clear what my options might be ... until I remembered my first sense of calling, which was to be a missionary. The clarity which emerged out of this season of unrest led to becoming a Church & Community Worker with the General Board of Global Ministries of the United Methodist Church. It was the GBGM which appointed me to direct an Older Adult Day Care in Birmingham, Alabama. This is where I served for 2 ½ years, until I was transferred to Lancaster, Pennsylvania.

While transitioning to Lancaster, I wondered about the need for a missionary in Lancaster, PA. It's not a major metropolitan area. But in the process of interviewing, I learned that the inner city of Lancaster indeed has the same issues found a larger urban area – poverty, hunger, homelessness, etc. Following my interview, which resulted in my hire, I prepared for my move to PA.

For 20 years my position in Lancaster turned out to be an amazingly good fit. During my early years in this position, our project was named LUMINA, which is the Latin word for LIGHT. Three areas of focus had already been established for this mission throughout Lancaster County: 1.) A food bank; 2.) A ministry with children & youth; and 3.) The administration of a discretionary fund for emergency assistance. I'd been with LUMINA a few years when we added a nutrition education ministry known as "SuperCupboard." For 20 years my responsibilities included speaking at local churches, sharing the Good News of the Gospel, and soliciting financial and personal support. As Executive Director, I got to recruit and provide orientation for staff and volunteers. I was privileged to work with some capable administrative assistants and board members, as well as some amazing volunteers and participants in our program ministries.

It was during my season with LUMINA that God brought my husband into my life. I could not ask for a more supportive spouse. Early on in our marriage, when I was upset about some of our differences, he asked, *"And why would I have wanted to marry someone just like me?"* One of his many gifts is knowing how to ask the right question at the right time! While we are not "on the same page" about everything, our marriage, like my ministry, is a calling, and an affirmation of God's creativity.

When it came time for me to move on from LUMINA, another Executive Director was hired. I knew and affirmed the person who was hired and continued to believe that this is God's Mission. What I did not know at the time was what the future would hold for me. I applied and interviewed for 3 different positions with social service agencies. None of them worked out. Then one day, when I least expected it, I received a call from the Senior Pastor of Lancaster: Covenant UMC. He said, *"We're looking for an interim Pastor of Visitation and Outreach at Covenant, and I wondered if you would be interested?"* I never cease to be amazed at how God uses both my strengths and weaknesses!

During the first year, not knowing how this church would be re-configuring their staff and not knowing how long God would use me in this ministry, I applied for a position with our Eastern

PA Conference of the UMC to serve as part time Director of Development for our Camps and Conferences, I applied, interviewed and was surprised to be hired for this position! The challenges of this position taught me that Development is not one of my greatest strengths. It also taught me that, in God's economy no experience is ever wasted. I wrote a few grants; met monthly with the Camp & Retreat Ministry (CRM) Board of Directors; wrote thank you notes for contributions received; submitted articles for our monthly newsletter and had many conversations with my supervisor and others, who reminded me that this work is not easy and it takes time.

While in this position, I had an important conversation with my husband's stepson and his wife. I shared my disappointment that this position didn't seem to be a very good "fit" for me. Brian said, *"Well, it's not all up to you, you know."* **And Mary said,** *"Don't Sell Yourself SHORT!"* **It was this conversation which led me to title my story, "NOT Selling Myself SHORT!"**

One morning in 2016, as I was driving to work, a message came to me. Though it was not audible, it might as well have been. The message was, "You're going to need to be bold today." I thought, Who, me?! Bold?! Why? About what?! That day I met up with a sister in Christ, Pastor Dorcas. Originally from Sierra Leone, Dorcas was pastoring a small membership church in our area at the time. I had heard that God was calling her to return to her native country to start an orphanage for children whose parents were victims of the Ebola outbreak in 2014-2015. We talked, hugged and prayed. Then she looked into my eyes and said, *"But, Pastor Sally, someone has to take my church."* I asked if she had time to tell me about her church. She did. Following our conversation, I sent an e-mail to my District Superintendent (supervisor of clergy), asking if I might serve this church. He replied, "Thank you for serving God. Please give me time to pray and talk with our Bishop." The next morning we were in a meeting together. After this meeting, he asked if we could talk. Within the next two months, I resigned from my conference position and was appointed to pastor Newtown UMC.

This appointment did not have a specific time frame. As it turns out, during the year and a half that I served NUMC, God used me to "stand in the gap." My husband and I grew to love this small membership, mission-minded congregation. The feelings were mutual. In fact, they spoiled us! When preaching every Sunday became stressful, and a much younger pastor became available, I moved on and he was appointed to this position. We have continued to savor a number of special friendships formed there.

Next came an opportunity to serve at Our Home of Hope, a residence for adults, male and female, who are mentally challenged and need a safe and structured living environment. I connected very quickly with the residents. I also enjoyed some domestic tasks which I don't often do at home, such as cleaning, laundry, assisting residents with bathing, helping to serve meals and clearing the tables. Regrettably, I didn't connect well with some of the staff. It turned out that *this* job was not what I had hoped it would be.

Next I learned that our piano tuner was looking for someone to help with some office work. A friend who had worked with him for many years was moving to another state. It was a part time position. My co-worker was a person with Bipolar Disorder.

previously known as manic depression. Though I didn't realize it while I was growing up, my mother also may have lived with this challenge. In addition to making phone calls and helping with bookkeeping, I tried to support Jeff with active listening when he was eager to talk. This position turned out to be short term.

All of these positions since LUMINA were part time, while I also continued at Covenant UMC part time. I addition, I have held one volunteer position as pianist at a small independent church near my home. I realize this might be confusing - but variety is the spice of life!

LIVING THROUGH UPS AND DOWNS

I STRIVE TO MAINTAIN a realistic outlook and to live a balanced life. Life is a mix of good and bad, a mix of ease and difficulty, a mix of ups and downs. Some times are bitter. Other times are better. Sometimes are sweet. Other times are bittersweet. Though I have not had the pleasure of meeting the woman who wrote the following food for thought, when I read it, I thought, "This speaks to me. I want it to be a part of my life story." I want to give her credit, and I hope it speaks to you, too:

<u>A TIME OF UPS & DOWNS</u>
Hope C. Oberhelman

Life is a time of ups and downs, and moments of despair.
But when the hours begin to pass, we find joy waiting there ...
Life is a time of ups and downs, and happiness and pain.
The days are often full of sun, but are sometimes wet with rain ...

Life is a time of ups and downs, and worlds of hope and care.
It is a time of solitude, and quiet thoughts and prayer ...
Life is a time of ups and downs, but love is all around,
So, let us live each day in peace, that beauty may be found!

During my junior high years, I had a boyfriend who sometimes walked me home. One day he invited me to go with him to a dance at our junior high school. He nicknamed me, "Compact," which I thought was rather clever. This turned out to be an early adolescent "crush." At our class' 50th celebration, I felt sad as I learned that he was deceased.

As a sophomore in high school, I took Driver Education. I was excited about learning to drive. Our class was required to learn how to drive cars with either a manual or an automatic transmission. My instructor told my mother that I might never be able to drive. Thankfully, auto manufacturers have figured out how to provide alternatives for persons who are short in stature, as well as persons with other physical challenges.

At a retreat which I attended as a young adult, our topic was the Psalms. As a writing assignment, I chose to paraphrase Psalm 13: A Prayer for Deliverance, It begins, *"How long, O Lord? Will you forget me forever ...?"* At that time, I was wondering how long I would have to wait to find a life partner.

It took several years for me to feel content with being single. I do believe that marriage isn't necessarily for everyone. During my mid to late forties, the time came when my prayers changed from being reserved in asking God for a husband to praying, *"God, if it's your will for me to be single for the rest of my life, then please help me to accept that."* I gradually became more relaxed, finding meaning and purpose in my single life, in my ministry and mission, and in my community involvement.

Then, when I least expected it, my husband came into my life. Bruce doesn't mind that I'm *short*. His mother, grandmother, and Aunt Betty were all just slightly taller than I. I am blessed that he continues to understand, *"It's what's inside that counts."*

Bruce was married before. Sadly, his first wife died of ovarian cancer. We knew each other, and I knew his parents as well. Our church family prayerfully supported Bruce and Teresa through her illness. We rejoiced when she had a period of remission and wept when her cancer came back. This time it had spread to her liver. During their 2 ½ years of marriage, she was ill and receiving cancer treatments most of the time

When Teresa died, I felt compassion for Bruce. He was grieving, and not looking to get into another committed relationship right away. However, he was looking for a friend to do things with. Our first "date" was on a Friday evening, when we went out to eat. After dinner, he hosted a fun time with mutual friends who came to his house to play table games. I was included in this "game night." This was just before Thanksgiving. That night I thought, *"I need to help this man get through the holidays."* I had attended Teresa's funeral as a friend, never thinking that Bruce and I would end up together. We dated for 2 years and were engaged for another eleven months before being married. I became serious before he did. I wish I could say I was patient during this time, but I do understand how wise it was of him to not rush the grieving process.

REACHING OUT

IF YOU SHARE my diagnosis of Turner Syndrome, I want to encourage you to enjoy your life journey. I invite you to remember, "Don't Sell Yourself Short." I invite you to remember, "Life's Too Short" to wish you were any other way just than the way you are.

First of all, I've found it to be extremely helpful to talk with other people about what it's like to live with TS. I encourage you to reach out to others with the questions you are asking, or which life with TS is asking of you. For example, TS is asking of me, "Why do I get moody sometimes?" The answer to that one is, many people with T.S. experience, as a side effect, hypothyroidism (an underactive thyroid gland.) There are hormones involved. This can be regulated with medication. I've learned that if I forget to take my thyroid medication, it definitely affects my mood. I'll be forever grateful for my family and friends who are willing to bear with me through these mood swings!

If you haven't already done so, I encourage you to connect with The Turner Syndrome Society of the United States (TSSUS). I have found their Mission & Vision statements to be inspiring:

Our Mission: *The Turner Syndrome Society of the United States advances knowledge, facilitates research, and provides support for all touched by Turner Syndrome.*

Our Vision: *Every girl and woman with Turner syndrome will have cutting edge health care ensuring the best quality of life.*

I encourage you to check out their web site: www.turnersyndrome.org.

STANDING ON THE PROMISES

*I*N A MONTHLY session with my Spiritual Director, I found the courage (or it found me) to mention the possibility of writing my life story. He said, *"You're a good writer, and you are helping people here and now. If you would write your life story, you could help more people for many years to come."*

It's helped me to consider that many of the things which have come into my life which I saw as limitations are the very things that have stretched me and led to significant personal growth, on the inside, where it really counts.

I'm grateful that my life journey has led me to claim a personal mission **"To live in solidarity with those who are marginalized by our society."**

In addition, three things have emerged for me as personal guidelines:

1. "<u>Don't</u> get in a yank." <u>Do</u> take your time.
2. "<u>Don't</u> over-extend." <u>Do</u> think it through.

3. Remember, "<u>God</u> is the potter. <u>You</u> are the clay."

These things have emerged as core values:

1. Authenticity
2. Compassion
3. Partnership

As these priorities have emerged, my faith has been undergirded by the support of a Covenant Group to which I've belonged since 1988. This resulted from serving on our denomination's General Board of Discipleship (GBOD). Our group is composed of members from throughout the US. We have seen one another through an amazing mix of life changes, including divorce; marriage; the death of one of our members; the death of other loved ones, and the election of one of our members to the episcopacy, as a Bishop of our denomination. By the time we all had served our terms on GBOD, we realized how important we had become to one another. As a result, we began meeting in person every 12 to 18 months. We took turns hosting. During 2020, given the limitations placed upon our lives by the coronavirus, we've been unable to meet in person. Instead, we've been meeting monthly on zoom. We are grateful for this technology, which enables us to keep in touch.

Life is a mix. So why not take each day as it comes? Why not share the passions and talents which make us the unique persons that we were created to be? It's my hope and prayer that your life journey is and will continue to be fruitful, that stumbling blocks will become steppingstones, and that there will always be someone or something to pick you up when you fall. May all of these things fit together like the pieces of a puzzle in *your* life, so that you may not only survive, but thrive!!!

Earlier in my life, I sometimes thought that I was insignificant **I used to sell myself short.** Since I figure that thoughts like this come into my life for a reason, I like to share them! This one is anonymous, or I would certainly give the credit do:

> You may think that you are
> completely insignificant in this world.
> But someone drinks coffee every morning
> from their favorite cup that you gave them.
> Someone heard a song on the radio
> that reminded them of you.
> Someone read the book you recommended,
> and plunged headfirst into it.
> Someone remembered your joke
> and smiled, returning home from work
> in the evening.
> Someone loves himself (or herself) a little more,
> because you gave them a compliment.
> Never think that you have no influence
> whatsoever. Your trace, which you leave behind
> with even a few good deeds,
> cannot be erased.

I am extremely grateful for each person who has shown interest in and taken the time to read my story.

Regardless of your life situation, including your unique set of assets and challenges, if our paths should cross at any time in any way, I would love to have the opportunity to ask you, I'm "NOT Selling Myself Short". HOW ABOUT YOU?!

ACKNOWLEDGEMENTS

THIS BOOK HAS evolved over about 18 months. This includes not only writing but sharing drafts at various stages of composition. I have been blessed with 2 mentors in my life - Dr. David Lowes Watson and Ruth Daugherty. Another friend, Barbara Hough Hueskin, helped with editing, using her professional experience with editing. I hesitate to mention every friend who has read my story and given feedback, because I do not want to omit anyone. You know who you are, and I invite you to include yourself in this number.

I have been assigned a series of consultants by Xulon Press to work with me on my personal project. As a first time author, I deeply appreciate every bit of guidance and encouragement.

Kudos ALWAYS to my husband, Bruce R. Ott, for being such a supportive spouse!

ABOUT THE AUTHOR...

NOT SELLING MYSELF SHORT:
One Woman's Journey with Turner Syndrome

*S*ALLY WISNER OTT is an Ordained Elder in the United Methodist Church. Diagnosed at age 8 with a genetic condition called Turner Syndrome, she has been reflecting significantly more in retirement than before on how "TS" has shaped her life and faith. She has been a staff person in several local churches, in various roles. Currently she serves as Pastor of Visitation and Outreach at Covenant United Methodist Church is in Lancaster, PA. She enjoys swimming, journaling, game nights with friends, working word puzzles in a daily newspaper, reading *and now writing!* She describes the process of writing her life story as "Exhilarating and Exhausting."

She lives in Lititz, Pennsylvania, with her husband, Bruce, and their pet rabbit, Honey Bunny Ott.